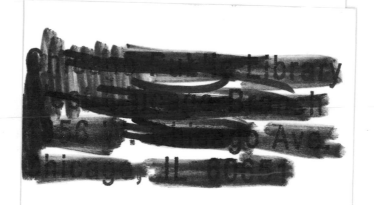

The Great Chicago Fire

CORNERSTONES OF FREEDOM

SECOND SERIES

R. Conrad Stein

Children's Press®
A Division of Scholastic Inc.
New York • Toronto • London • Auckland • Sydney
Mexico City • New Delhi • Hong Kong
Danbury, Connecticut

Photographs © 2005: Art Resource, NY/Scala: 3; Chicago Historical Society (original black and white photographs color tinted by permission): 41, 45 right (C. D. Arnold/ICHi-23162), 36 (Copelin & Hine/ICHi-02773), 23 (Copelin/ICHi-00718), 7 (D. F. Fabronius/I CHi-05629), 26 (George P. A. Healy/P&S-1901.0001), 9 (Hesler/I CHi-05734), 4, 44 left (Lovejoy & Foster/ICHi-02737), 22 (Frank Luzerne/ICHi-02929), 14 (Moss Eng. Co./ICHi-00442), 30 (R. P. Studley Company, St. Louis/ICHi-14894), 25 (Alfred R. Waud/ICHi-37788), 11 (DIA-1959.399), 34 (ICHi-02859), 28 (ICHi-02881), 20 (ICHi-02897), 39 (ICHi-10864), 12 (ICHi-31916); Corbis Images: cover top, 5, 13, 19, 21, 35, 37, 44 right (Bettmann), 24 (Kevin Fleming), 27, 29 (Robert Holmes), 40 (Joseph Sohm/ChromoSohn Inc.), 38, 45 left (Underwood & Underwood), 8 (E. Whitefield), 31; Getty Images: cover bottom, 33 (Oscar Gustav Rejlander/Hulton Archive); North Wind Picture Archives: 10, 16, 17; Stock Montage, Inc.: 6, 15; Wisconsin Historical Society/Mel Kishner: 32.

Library of Congress Cataloging-in-Publication Data
Stein, R. Conrad.
 The Great Chicago Fire / R. Conrad Stein.
     p. cm. — (Cornerstones of freedom. Second series)
  Includes bibliographical references and index.
  ISBN 0-516-23640-7
  1. Great Fire, Chicago, Ill., 1871—Juvenile literature. 2. Fires—Illinois—Chicago—History—19th century—Juvenile literature.
3. Chicago (Ill.)—History—To 1875—Juvenile literature. I. Title.
II. Series.
  F548.42.S76 2005
  977.3'11041—dc22   2004018087

1 2 3 4 5 6 7 8 9 10 R 14 13 12 11 10 09 08 07 06 05

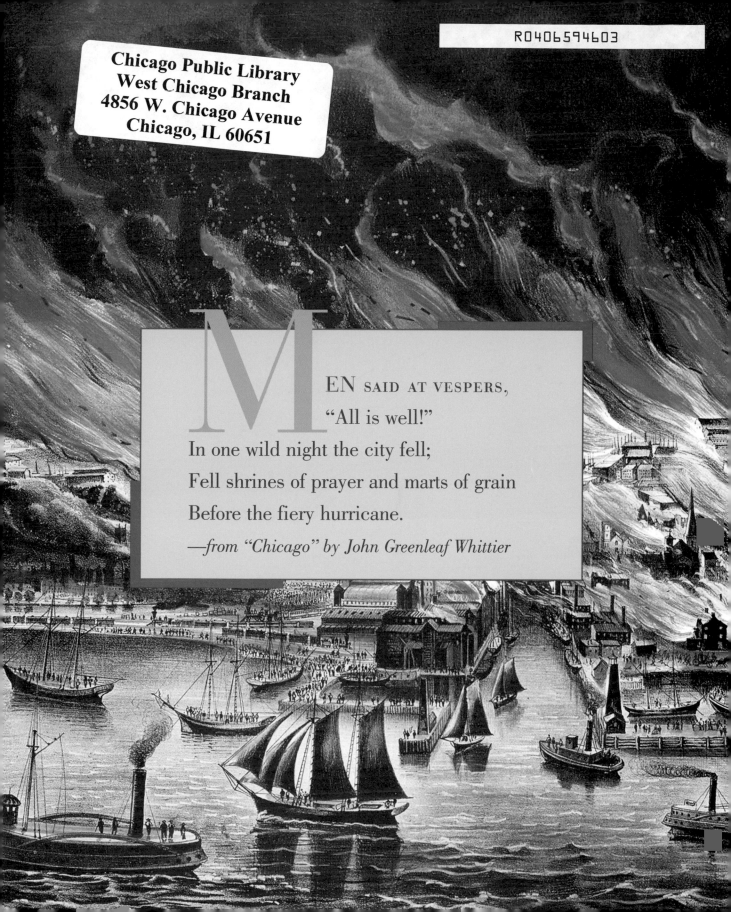

MEN SAID AT VESPERS,
"All is well!"
In one wild night the city fell;
Fell shrines of prayer and marts of grain
Before the fiery hurricane.
—*from "Chicago" by John Greenleaf Whittier*

The O'Leary house was located at 137 DeKoven Street. The barn was behind the cottage.

A WINDY SUNDAY NIGHT

Catherine and Patrick O'Leary were respected members of Chicago's Irish immigrant community. They owned a small cottage at 137 DeKoven Street, where they raised three children. Patrick had fought for the Union during the Civil War and now worked as a laborer. Catherine tended cows in a barn behind their house. She supplied the neighborhood with fresh milk. No one could have dreamed that this perfectly average family would be blamed for one of the greatest disasters ever to strike a city in the United States.

It was Sunday evening, October 8, 1871. Daniel Sullivan, an old family friend, knocked on the O'Leary's door. Sullivan hoped to chat and perhaps play cards. But Mr. and Mrs. O'Leary said they were tired and ready for bed. So Sullivan went outside and sat on a step overlooking the O'Leary house.

It was a warm and windy night. As usual the weather was dry. Just before 9:00 P.M. Sullivan noticed an orange glow near the O'Leary's barn. In those days, backyard barns holding cows, horses, and chickens were common. Naturally the barns were loaded with hay. As Sullivan got closer, he saw flames licking at its sides. He yelled out, "Fire! Fire!"

Taken in 1934, this picture shows a much later view of DeKoven Street, where the fire began.

Neighbors opened their windows and came out onto the street. At first, the fire offered a dash of excitement on a lazy Sunday night. People believed that firefighters would soon arrive and put out the flames, just as they always did. Certainly no one suspected this fire would end up burning down most of the city. That couldn't happen in Chicago, a city that had known nothing but spectacular progress in its brief history.

★ ★ ★ ★

Fort Dearborn, the U.S. Army post at the mouth of the Chicago River, was peaceful for several years.

A CITY BLOSSOMS

Chicago was once swampland where a slow-moving river emptied into Lake Michigan. Local Potawatomi Indians called the river the Checagou, which is thought to mean "wild onion place."

In 1782, a man named Jean Baptiste Point du Sable established a trading post along the river. He bought furs from the American Indians. A U.S. Army post called Fort Dearborn was built on the grounds in 1803. The fort was mostly peaceful until 1812. In August, an attack by the Potawatomi killed many soldiers and settlers. This attack became known as the

Fort Dearborn Massacre. By the early 1830s, problems with the American Indians had been resolved to the advantage of the settlers, and Chicago was ripe for expansion.

Chicago officially became a town early in 1833. At the time, it was a muddy little settlement with fewer than two hundred people. But it wasn't long before Chicago began to spread out over the flat prairie lands.

In less than thirty years, Chicago had 100,000 residents. A visitor named Joseph Jefferson stepped off a Lake Michigan steamer in 1837. He reported, "Off we go ashore and walk through the busy little town . . . people hurrying to and from, frame buildings going up, board sidewalks going down, new hotels, new churches, new theaters, everything new. Saw and hammer—saw, saw, bang, bang."

This is one artist's view of how Chicago may have looked in the 1820s, before a large number of settlers arrived.

CHICAGO'S POPULATION GROWTH BEFORE THE FIRE	
Year	Population
1830	100
1840	4,470
1850	29,963
1860	112,172
1870	298,977

★ ★ ★ ★

Location was the key to Chicago's growth. The city lay halfway between the East Coast and the expanding western regions. Livestock, wheat, and other farm goods shipped from the West to big cities in the East were often routed through Chicago. With its fine harbor on Lake Michigan, Chicago served thousands of ships.

The first railroad lines reached Chicago in 1848. In less than ten years, the Chicago region had 3,000 miles (4,827 kilometers) of track. It was the world's busiest railroad center.

Industry was booming, too. Chicago's factories turned out farm tools and railroad equipment. Writer Noah Brooks proclaimed, "Here on the shore of Lake Michigan has risen a great and growing city, worthy to bear the title of the Empire City of the West."

Chicago's success was partly because of its location. Ships and barges could easily reach the area by way of Lake Michigan and the Chicago River.

PINEWOOD AND SLUMS

Chicago paid a price for its fabulous growth. Social services for the poor were scarce. Safety standards for building construction were largely ignored to allow for runaway expansion.

More than half of Chicago's residents were foreign-born. Most came from Europe. They held low-paying jobs and lived in whatever housing they could afford. Spreading out from downtown were some of the nation's worst slums. In the slums, rows of wooden cottages were built side-by-side with only narrow walkways between them. Construction was quick and poorly done. Older cottages leaned toward each other to the point where roofs almost touched. A visiting journalist called the immigrants' houses "miserable **hovels**."

Speed was the rule when it came to building houses in Chicago. In 1871, the city had about 59,000 structures, including houses, hotels, department stores, factories, and churches. Seven out of eight of these buildings were made of wood.

In 1858, a photographer named Alexander Hesler took pictures of every part of Chicago, as seen from the top of the Courthouse. This view shows the northern part of the city.

These wooden structures on the dock were typical of many buildings in Chicago at the time of the fire.

Wood from pine trees was plentiful in the Midwest. Wooden buildings could be constructed in far less time than brick structures. A new kind of house, called the balloon house, was developed in Chicago in the 1840s. A balloon house was made from a frame of wooden beams covered over with boards. These houses were often hammered together in a week. Early Chicago could be called a pinewood city. It even had 500 miles (805 km) of wooden sidewalks.

* ✦ ✦ ✦

Fires were common in the hastily constructed wooden neighborhoods. Records show that 515 fires were reported in the year 1868 alone. This was a much higher rate than in communities with mostly brick buildings. In 1870, an average of two fires a day broke out somewhere in the city.

Chicago city leaders tried to address this problem. The nation's most modern fire-detection system was created as a result. The city set up 172 iron fire-alarm boxes. When a fire was discovered, a person opened a door on the box and pulled a lever. An electric signal alerted the fire department and gave the exact location of the blaze. To prevent false alarms, the boxes were locked, and keys were given to responsible citizens, usually storekeepers who lived nearby. In addition, men were posted as fire-watchers on high roofs, including the bell tower of the courthouse building downtown. This system allowed fire department crews to speed to a fire as quickly as possible.

Still, weather conditions left Chicago at risk to a large-scale fire. A **drought** gripped the entire Midwest in 1871. Only 1 inch (2.5 centimeters) of rain had fallen between July 4 and October 9. In Chicago, the trees lost their leaves in mid-August. Wind-blown dry leaves piled high against wooden fences and alongside houses. In October 1871, the *Chicago Tribune* reported, "The absence of rain has left everything in so **flammable** a condition that a spark might set a fire which would sweep from end to end of the city."

This was one of many fire alarms throughout the city by the 1860s. The alarms were linked to a main alarm office in the courthouse.

11

This fire engine, the *R. A. Williams,* belonged to the Chicago Fire Department in the mid-1800s.

THE INFERNO BEGINS

Everything went wrong for Chicago on the night of October 8, 1871. A terrible fire the day before had destroyed four square blocks on the city's South Side. It took seventeen hours for firefighters to battle that blaze. They were exhausted and fire engines were in need of repair. The fire on DeKoven Street could not have come at a worse time.

Flames shot out from the O'Leary's barn. The barn held 3 tons of dry hay, which burned with an intense fury. Fire raced over dry leaves and grass to ignite a nearby wooden fence. A neighbor's barn was showered with sparks and burst into flames. Winds sent burning sticks and red-hot

As a result of a rumor that became a popular legend thanks to interest from the press, many Chicagoans believed that the fire started when Mrs. O'Leary's cow kicked over a lantern in the DeKoven Street barn.

13

The Courthouse was built in the 1850s in the downtown Chicago area. At the time of the fire, a watchman was on duty in the cupola at the top of the building.

ashes to the rooftops of other houses. Everyone in the crowd on DeKoven Street asked, "Where's the fire department?"

The watchman on duty at the courthouse tower saw the blaze. He quickly sent horse-driven fire wagons on their way. However, he directed them to a spot almost 1 mile (1.6 km) from the O'Leary's barn.

Meanwhile, William Lee, who lived near DeKoven Street, ran to Goll's drugstore to report the fire. Bruno Goll had the key to the neighborhood fire-alarm box. Goll assured Lee there was no need to pull the alarm lever because he had already seen fire wagons rumbling down the street—the same wagons that were headed to the wrong place. Because of these mistakes, the fire was not properly reported. It took almost forty-five minutes for major units of the Chicago Fire Department to reach DeKoven Street. By that time, the fire was a raging inferno.

Riding on strong winds, the fire tore through one neighborhood of wooden cottages after another. Fire companies lined up their wagons and pumped water through hoses to

Thousands of people crowded the bridges in an effort to escape the fire.

DON'T BLAME THE COW

Soon after the fire started, a rumor spread across Chicago. People said that the fire was caused by an Irish immigrant named Mrs. O'Leary, whose cow accidentally kicked over a kerosene lamp. (Kerosene is a liquid fuel that produces a bright flame.) This story allowed people to blame the fire on the Irish newcomers, who were not popular among well-to-do Chicagoans. There was no evidence that this story was true, but no matter. Generations of Americans grew up believing the Great Chicago Fire was started by Mrs. O'Leary, her cow, and a lantern.

★ ★ ★ ★

block the fire's advance. But winds sent sparks and cinders over the heads of the firefighters, carrying the blaze to their rear. One firefighter said, "You couldn't see anything over you but fire. That night the wind and the fire were the same."

Masses of terrified people ran from the flames. Hundreds crowded onto bridges at the south branch of the Chicago River. Those who could not see because of the smoke followed the clanging of the courthouse fire-alarm bell. People thought they would find

The fire blew across the Chicago River, sending nearby buildings and boats into flames.

16

safety over the bridges. *Surely,* they thought, *the fire could not leap over the river.*

At about 11:30 P.M., the wall of flame reached the south branch of the Chicago River. Burning **embers**, described as a "red rain," blew across the water. A horse stable on the opposite side went up in smoke. Gone were the hopes that the river would serve as a natural **barrier** to the fire. The fire was now a monster that grew stronger and more fierce as it fed.

Chicagoans tried to outrun the fire as flames engulfed Courthouse Square.

Beyond the river stood an immigrant slum known as Conley's Patch. At first, some drunken slum residents danced in the street at the site of the flames. But the roar of the fire and the powerful heat quickly brought them to their senses. Men and women rushed into their houses and grabbed whatever they could carry. Then they joined the crowds fleeing the fire.

A REPORTER'S VIEWS

A newspaper writer named Joseph Chamberlain was at the scene when the fire hit Conley's Patch. Chamberlain regarded the neighborhood people as ignorant foreigners. His reporting reflected this attitude:

On that night [Conley's Patch] was crowded with people [pouring] out of the thickly settled locality between Jefferson Street and the river. The wretched female inhabitants were rushing out almost naked, imploring spectators to help them with their burdens of bed quilts, cane-bottomed chairs, iron kettles, etc. . . . [A]ll was confusion.

THE DEVIL'S FIRE

The fire moved in two directions: east toward the lake and north toward the downtown business district. Those who made their way west reached relative safety. In fact, some Chicago neighborhoods were left untouched by the Great Fire. But on this night of chaos and terror, no one could predict what course the fire would take.

Crowds of people raced northward ahead of the flames. Some screamed in mortal fear. Others chanted prayers. The wall of fire was now 1,000 feet (305 meters) wide and 100 feet (30.5 m) high. In some sections, it moved as fast as a man can run. Elderly and sick people were the first to die. Some were trampled by the crowd. Others were caught by the flames and burned to death.

Firefighters continued spraying water on buildings. But howling winds blew so hard that the water streaming from the hoses backed up and splashed into the faces of the fire-

Panicked, the residents of threatened neighborhoods rushed into the streets with their belongings.

fighters. Volunteer citizens joined the fire crews. They tore down wooden fences and sheds to keep flammable material from the fire's path. Crews exploded buildings to create fire-breaks, or gaps in the path of the flames. But nothing stopped the fire's advance. One firefighter was heard to say, "This is the devil's own fire."

Middle-class and rich downtown residents soon joined the fleeing masses. Horse-drawn wagons rushed through the streets. One eyewitness said,

The horses, maddened by the heat and noise, and irritated by the falling sparks, neighed and screamed with

19

*fright and anger, and roared and kicked and bit each other. . . . Dogs ran hither and thither, howling dismally. Great brown rats, with beadlike eyes, were **ferreted** out from under the sidewalks by the flames, and scurried down the streets.*

SINNERS AND SAINTS

Panic took hold in the downtown neighborhoods that lay ahead of the fire's path. A great yellow glow to the south told everyone their houses and buildings would be destroyed. Storekeepers waited until the last moment, then locked their stores to join the crowds moving north. In some places,

Some newspaper reports emphasized criminal acts that took place during the fire. Illustrations such as these showed men breaking into saloons.

looters braved the approaching flames. They broke into the stores to steal food, liquor, jewelry, and anything else they could carry.

Sidewalk preachers shouted that this disaster was God's punishment of the sinful people of Chicago. They compared the flames in Chicago to the fire of Hell. Yet only a few Chicagoans acted the role of sinners that night. Newspaper accounts later told of criminals stalking the streets "like vultures in search of prey." Most of those stories proved to be greatly **exaggerated.** One reporter, Alfred L. Sewell, wrote, "There was little of either theft or robbery."

For every criminal there were hundreds of heroes. Some people dropped their household goods to carry

Families huddled in despair next to their belongings.

injured strangers to safety. Men and women rushed into smoky buildings to rescue those who were trapped. Newspaper editor Horace White wrote, "I saw a great many kindly acts done as we moved along. The poor helped the

For the most part, Chicagoans did what they could to help one another escape the massive fire.

★ ★ ★ ★

rich and the rich helped the poor (if anyone could be called rich at such a time)."

An artist named John R. Chapman tried to sketch the fire in all its fury. Chapman failed to complete his drawing because the flames were upon him so suddenly. Around him, fleeing people screamed, and the great fire roared. "[The] frightful **discord** of sounds will live in memory while life shall last," said Chapman. He was one of the lucky ones who managed to escape the fire and board a train heading out of town. On the train Chapman wrote, "Forty miles away we still saw the brilliant flames looming above the doomed city."

At 1:30 A.M., the courthouse in the center of the city caught fire. Prisoners in the courthouse jail downstairs rattled the bars of their cells until jailers released them. Robbers and brawlers were free to join the crowds on the streets. In less than an hour, the courthouse bell, still sounding its alarm, fell five stories to the ground. It was finally silent.

The blaze spread to the post office, to the banks, and to the train stations. Field and Leiter's department store also burned even though it was advertised as being "completely fireproof."

As the blaze spread, the elegant Grand Pacific Hotel became engulfed in flames. This hotel held one of Chicago's first elevators, a device that was called "a vertical railroad to connect all floors."

Today, the Drake Hotel is a Chicago landmark.

JOHN DRAKE'S HUNCH

John Drake owned a hotel in the city. When his own hotel caught fire, Drake moved north with the masses. On a hunch, he entered another hotel on Michigan Avenue. Guessing the flames would not reach that part of Michigan Avenue, Drake offered to buy it. The hotel owner thought that his place would soon be reduced to ashes, so he accepted the offer. As it turned out, the flames did not touch the Michigan Avenue hotel. Drake made a fortune by owning the only first-class hotel to survive the fire.

THE LAST REFUGE

Raging and roaring, the fire advanced through the downtown streets. Ahead of its path, the crowds marched north, seeking safe ground. Almost everyone carried something—a rolled-up carpet or a prized lamp. Children clutched a toy soldier, a doll, or perhaps a Sunday dress. That night all Chicagoans were the same, wealthy or not.

This sketch by Alfred R. Waud shows people fleeing from the burning city with their belongings. Waud created more than thirty pictures of the fire.

William Ogden was mayor of Chicago from 1837 to 1838. Although Ogden later moved to New York, he still owned a home in Chicago, which was destroyed by the great fire.

★ ★ ★ ★

Years afterward, survivors would recall that the winds sang eerie songs. Some said the winds "howled," others claimed they "screamed." Still others said they "moaned." William Ogden, an ex-mayor and a Chicago pioneer, wrote, "The fire was the fiercest Tornado of Wind ever known to blow here." The fire actually produced the strong winds by sucking air into its center, creating tremendous drafts at ground level. Caught in this windswept firestorm was a woman named Aurelia King. King rushed along the smoke-filled streets with her two small children in hand. "You could not conceive of anything more fearful. I fled with my children clinging to me, fled literally in a shower of fire. . . . The wind was like a tornado and I held fast to my little ones, fearing they would be lifted from my sight. . . ."

Once more, Chicago River bridges were scenes of **bedlam** as people and horsecarts crowded over them. The escapees crossed the main branch of the Chicago River, which separated downtown from the North Side. This time, few Chicagoans expected the river to stop the fire's advance.

A modern-day view of Lincoln Park.

Even before the inferno reached the riverbanks, winds sent **firebrands** sweeping across the water. Accounts claimed that the North Side section burned faster than downtown did.

Because the fire moved so quickly over the northern district, thousands of people became trapped on the city's lakefront. Today, that section is home to fashionable Lincoln Park and the Oak Street Beach. On the night of October 8 and the morning of October 9, 1871, it was refuge to huddled men, women, and children. These frightened people watched their city disappear under what appeared to be an ocean of flames.

Many Chicagoans looked for safety in Lincoln Park, part of which was used as a cemetery.

Hundreds of people walked into the cooling lake waters. There they stood in water up to their necks. Some reports said the heat set fire to the hair of people standing in the waters. For a woman named Del Moore, this last refuge in the lake was the most awful aspect of the fire. "Such a scene of horror and terror I cannot make you imagine," she said in a letter to her parents. "I begged [my husband] Gus if I took fire to put me in the Lake and drown me, not let me burn to death."

THE WATER TOWER

Today, the Water Tower remains a proud symbol of the city. The building rises on Michigan Avenue, a little less than 1 mile (1.6 km) from the Chicago River. This stretch of Michigan Avenue is so elegant that it is called Chicago's "Magnificent Mile."

The Water Tower survived the great fire, and today it is an important city landmark.

Just after 6:00 A.M. on October 10, the sun rose over Chicago. Through the smoke, the people crowded along the lake saw what they hailed as a miracle. Standing amid the wreckage was the Water Tower. The tower was part of a giant water-pumping system built in 1869. This morning the tower seemed like a ray of hope. Its unspoken message was "Chicago will survive."

29

A COSTLY TRAGEDY

The Great Chicago Fire lasted thirty hours. Records show the last structure destroyed by the fire was a doctor's house on Fullerton Avenue, far north of downtown. Beyond Fullerton Avenue were mostly woods and prairies. The Great Chicago Fire had destroyed the prime sections of the city. At ten o'clock on Monday evening, a welcome rain fell. Though the ruins would smolder for weeks, the fire was over.

MAP SHOWING THE BURNT DISTRICT IN CHICAGO,

Published for the benefit of the Relief Fund by 3.D EDITION. THE R.P. STUDLEY COMPANY, ST. LOUIS.

This is one of several maps that were created showing the burnt district in Chicago. The O'Leary cottage is at the upper left point. From there, the fire moved north (to the right) and east.

★ ★ ★ ★

Chicagoans counted their losses. They believed that between 200 and 300 people had been killed, but the true number of deaths was unknown. Many people were buried in the **debris,** their bodies reduced to ashes. Still others fell from bridges and were drowned.

About 18,000 buildings were destroyed. One hundred thousand people were left homeless. Surveys found that 1,600 stores, 60 factories, and 28 hotels were lost to the fire. Property damage was estimated at $200 million, a fortune in those days.

PESHTIGO, THE FORGOTTEN FIRE

Peshtigo, Wisconsin, is a logging town 250 miles (402 km) north of Chicago. On the night of October 8, 1871, residents of Peshtigo walked home from evening church services. In the distance, they heard a roar that sounded like a train and saw an eerie yellow light in the sky. Suddenly, from all sides, a great fire enveloped Peshtigo.

More than 1,200 people died in Peshtigo and in nearby communities. No one knows the cause of the fire. It spread with incredible speed because the ground in the surrounding forest was covered with wood chips left there by logging companies.

This terrible fire went largely unreported in national newspapers. Why? Because the Great Chicago Fire began the same night, at almost the same hour. The Chicago fire destroyed a large city, dominating newspaper headlines around the world. To this day, few people know of the Peshtigo fire, even though it took four times as many lives as did the disaster in Chicago.

★ ★ ★ ★

REBIRTH

The scene immediately after the Chicago fire was too gloomy for the senses to grasp. Where a great and vibrant city once stood lay a field of ashes. The second stanza of John Greenleaf Whittier's poem conveys the impact of this tremendous loss:

> *On threescore spires had sunset shone,*
> *Where ghostly sunrise looked on none.*
> *Men clasped each other's hands, and said:*
> *"The City of the West is dead."*

This illustration by Mel Kishner shows a family huddled in a field, hoping to escape the Peshtigo fire.

But of course Chicago was not dead. Even as the ashes smoldered, a store owner put a sign over the wreckage that was once his shop: ALL GONE BUT WIFE, CHILDREN, AND ENERGY! Two days after the fire, the *Chicago Tribune* wrote, "In the midst of a calamity without parallel in the world's history, looking upon the ashes of thirty years accumulations, the people of this once beautiful city have resolved that CHICAGO SHALL RISE AGAIN!"

Citizens from other parts of the country sprang into action. Relief trains stuffed with food and clothing arrived from New York and other cities. Volunteers from Cincinnati set up a soup kitchen and fed 3,500 people every day. A ladies' club from St. Louis donated blankets and mattresses to the homeless. Charities raised more than five million dollars to provide food and temporary shelter. From Washing-

William D. Kerfoot, owner of a real estate business in Chicago, reopened his business in this shanty the day after the fire, showing a determination that inspired many others.

AN UNUSUAL GIFT

An unusual gift to Chicago came from Queen Victoria of England. The queen led a drive to donate 7,000 books to the city. Those books were used to form Chicago's first free public library.

From across the country, contributions to help the fire victims poured into Chicago.

ton, President Ulysses S. Grant donated one thousand dollars to a Chicago relief agency.

In the end, it was the energy of Chicago's residents that rebuilt the city. Chicago businessman John Stephen Wright was one of many who saw a bright future. Days after the fire Wright's friend asked, "What do you think of the future of Chicago now?" Wright answered, "I will tell you what it is.

★ ★ ★ ★

Schock, Bigford & Company was thought to be the first store to reopen for business after the fire. It sold cigars, apples, cider, and other items from this street stand.

Chicago will have more men, more money, more business within five years than she would have without this fire."

WHAT WENT WRONG?

City leaders formed a **commission** to determine what caused the fire. They also wanted to find out what could be done to prevent another such tragedy. Investigators determined that the fire began in the barn in back of the O'Leary house on DeKoven Street. (The O'Leary barn was burnt to the ground, but the family's cottage suffered little damage.)

The commission was never able to tell exactly what started the blaze. One theory suggests the O'Leary family friend, Daniel Sullivan, went into the barn to drink whiskey and smoke his pipe. He then got careless with a match. Some reports say Sullivan confessed his guilt years later. Whatever the cause, the O'Leary family got the blame. Public hatred forced Catherine and Patrick O'Leary to move to rural Michigan. There, they lived more or less in hiding.

THE O'LEARY SITE TODAY

Today, the Chicago Fire Department Training Academy sits on the O'Leary homestead. A tall bronze statue, called *Pillar of Fire,* rises above what used to be the O'Leary barn.

This illustration from a November 1871 issue of *Harper's Weekly* shows the rebuilding of Chicago.

The Home Insurance Building in Chicago, designed by William Le Baron Jenney, is considered the first skyscraper in the United States.

The commission's findings were clear on one point: The fire spread out of control because many of Chicago's houses were poorly constructed. The city government passed laws stating that all new structures should be built using fire-resistant brick. The new Chicago was made of sturdy buildings designed to withstand fires.

At the time the city was being rebuilt, two new building developments were taking place: steel framing and the elevator. Steel framing allowed **architects** to design structures with a steel "skeleton" and build in more windows. The elevator allowed the towers to reach breathtaking heights.

The world's first true skyscraper was the ten-story Home Insurance Building. It was built in Chicago in 1884 by architect William Le Baron Jenney. Jenney and fellow architect Louis Sullivan headed what was called the Chicago School of Architecture. Chicago School designers created dozens of tall buildings with wide glass windows. High-rise office

William Le Baron Jenney

A modern view of downtown Chicago from Lake Michigan

POPULATION GROWTH AFTER THE FIRE

New residents continued to flock to Chicago, as these population figures show:

Year	Population
1880	503,185
1890	1,099,840
1900	1,698,575
1910	2,185,283
1920	2,701,705

buildings were developed largely in postfire Chicago. Twelve years after the fire, Mark Twain wrote:

It is hopeless for the occasional visitor to try to keep up with Chicago—she outgrows her prophecies faster than she can make them. She is always a **novelty;** *for she is never the Chicago you saw when you passed through the last time.*

In May 1893, thousands of visitors came to Chicago to attend the World's Fair. Called the World Columbian Exposition, the fair celebrated the four hundredth anniversary of Christopher Columbus's voyage.

Many people expected to see at least some damage left by the fire of twenty-two years earlier. Those visitors were disappointed. The city's rebuilding had been completed. Still, they heard a song called "From the Ruins Our City Shall Rise." The song was hastily written after the fire and was wildly popular afterward:

Ruins! Ruins! Far and wide.
From the river and the lake to the prairie side.
Dreary, dreary, the darkness falls,
While autumn winds moan through blackened walls.
But see! The bright rift in the cloud
And hear the great voice from shore!
Our city shall rise!
Yes, she shall rise!
Queen of the west once more!

Chicago hosted the World's Fair of 1893. The Court of Honor, shown here, was the main attraction.

Glossary

architect—a person who designs and directs the construction of buildings

barrier—a structure that serves to separate one thing from another

bedlam—extreme confusion

commission—a team of people working to investigate a matter

debris—the remains of something broken or destroyed

discord—a harsh mingling

drought—a shortage of rainfall

embers—small, glowing pieces of ash from a dying fire

evidence—information that serves as proof of something

exaggerated—expressed in an overstated manner

firebrands—pieces of burning wood

flammable—catches on fire easily

hovels—huts or sheds used as housing by the poor

novelty—something new and different than before

Timeline: The Great

1871

A drought grips the Midwest, creating very dry conditions.

OCTOBER 7
A huge fire, later called the Saturday Night Fire, destroys four square blocks on Chicago's South Side. Battling that blaze exhausts the fire crews and causes equipment breakdowns.

OCTOBER 8
Shortly before 9:00 P.M. a fire breaks out in the O'Leary barn on DeKoven Street.

OCTOBER 9
Just after midnight the fire begins to consume downtown.

OCTOBER 10
The fire finally burns itself out far north of downtown. A welcoming rain falls.

OCTOBER 11
The rebuilding of the city begins.

Chicago Fire

1880 | 1884 | 1890 | 1893

1880
Chicago's population exceeds 500,000.

1884
The world's first true skyscraper, the Home Insurance Building, is completed in downtown Chicago.

1890
Chicago's population exceeds one million people.

1893
Chicago hosts the World's Fair, called the World Columbian Exposition. Not a trace of fire damage can be seen in the city.

45

To Find Out More

BOOKS

Balcavage, Dynise. *The Great Chicago Fire.* Langhorne, PA: Chelsea House Publishers, 2001.

Ball, Jacqueline A. *Wildfire! The 1871 Peshtigo Firestorm.* New York: Bearport Publishing, 2005.

Murphy, Jim. *The Great Fire.* New York: Scholastic Books, 1995.

Stein, R. Conrad. *Chicago.* Danbury, CT: Children's Press, 1997.

ONLINE SITES

Chicago Historical Society, The Web of Memory
http://www.chicagohs.org/fire/

National Geographic Kids: Chicago Fire
http://www.nationalgeographic.com/ngkids/9809/chicago/

Index

Bold numbers indicate illustrations.

About the Author

R. Conrad Stein was born in Chicago and attended Chicago public schools. While growing up, he heard many stories about the Great Chicago Fire and grew fascinated with the subject. As a boy he, too, believed the Great Fire was caused by Mrs. O'Leary's cow. To prepare for writing this book, Stein walked the streets near the O'Leary barn site, followed the course of the fire, and tried to imagine the fear of thousands of people escaping the blaze.

At age eighteen, Stein joined the U.S. Marine Corps and served for three years. He then attended the University of Illinois, from which he graduated with a degree in history. Stein is a full-time author of books for young readers, and over the years he has published more than 150 titles. He is married to Deborah Kent, who is also a writer of books for young readers; they have a daughter, Janna. The Stein family still lives in Chicago.

S	N
卌 III	卌 卌
IIII	卌
	II